OUP-518

20·4 ·88

10

SECOND SIGHT

THREE CROWNS BOOKS

Arnold Apple: *Son of Guyana*
G. S. Sharat Chandra: *Heirloom*
John Pepper Clark: *Ozidi*
John Pepper Clark: *Three Plays*
Cowasjee & Kumar: *Modern Indian Short Stories*
Keki Daruwalla: *The Keeper of the Dead*
Keki Daruwalla: *Crossing of Rivers*
Manoranjan Das: *Wild Harvest*
J. C. de Graft: *Through a Film Darkly*
J. C. de Graft: *Sons and Daughters*
R. Sarif Easmon: *Dear Parent and Ogre*
Obi B. Egbuna: *Daughters of the Sun & Other Stories*
Nissim Ezekiel: *Hymns in Darkness*
Nissim Ezekiel: *Latter-Day Psalms*
Patrick Fernando: *Selected Poems*
Girish Karnad: *Hayavadana*
Girish Karnad: *Tughlaq*
Ashok Mahajan: *Goan Vignettes and Other Poems*
Jayanta Mahapatra: *Life Signs*
Howard McNaughton: *Contemporary New Zealand Plays*
Arvind Mehrotra: *Middle Earth*
U. R. Anantha Murthy: *Samskara: A Rite for a Dead Man*
Kalim Omar (ed.): *Wordfall: Three Pakistani Poets*
Sonny Oti: *Evangelist Jeremiah*
R. Parthasarathy (ed.): *Ten Twentieth-Century Indian Poets*
R. Parthasarathy: *Rough Passage*
A. K. Ramanujan: *Second Sight*
A. K. Ramanujan: *Selected Poems*
Raja Rao: *The Policeman and the Rose*
Ola Rotimi: *Ovonramwen Nogbaisi*
Ola Rotimi: *Kurunmi: An Historical Tragedy*
Ola Rotimi: *The Gods Are Not to Blame*
Badal Sircar: *Evam Indrajit*
Wole Soyinka: *Kongi's Harvest*
Wole Soyinka: *The Road*
Wole Soyinka: *The Lion and the Jewel*
Wole Soyinka: *A Dance of the Forests*
Vijay Tendulkar: *Silence! The Court Is in Session*
D. O. Umobuarie: *Black Justice*
Nirmal Verma: *Maya Darpan and Other Stories*
Joris Wartemberg: *The Corpse's Comedy*

SECOND SIGHT

A. K. Ramanujan

DELHI
OXFORD UNIVERSITY PRESS
OXFORD NEW YORK MELBOURNE
1986

Oxford University Press, Walton Street, Oxford OX2 6DP

OXFORD NEW YORK TORONTO
DELHI BOMBAY CALCUTTA MADRAS KARACHI
PETALING JAYA SINGAPORE HONG KONG TOKYO
NAIROBI DAR ES SALAAM CAPE TOWN
MELBOURNE AUCKLAND
and associates in
BEIRUT BERLIN IBADAN MEXICO CITY NICOSIA

Typeset and printed in India by P. K. Ghosh
at Eastend Printers, 3 Dr Suresh Sarkar Road, Calcutta 700014
and published by R. Dayal, Oxford University Press
YMCA Library Building, Jai Singh Road, New Delhi 110001

For
David Grene

CONTENTS

ACKNOWLEDGEMENTS

I am grateful to the editors of the following journals where earlier versions of these poems appeared:

Poetry (Chicago): 'In the Zoo', 'Ecology', 'Death and the Good Citizen'
The Carleton Miscellany: 'Chicago Zen'
The American Scholar: 'Extended Family'
Indian Literature: 'Elements of Composition', 'Looking for the Centre', 'No Amnesiac King'

The phrase 'Not on Thursday, not in Paris' on p. 43 alludes to César Vallejo's poem on his death, 'Black Stone on a White Stone.'

Elements of Composition

Composed as I am, like others,
    of elements on certain well-known lists,
father's seed and mother's egg

gathering earth, air, fire, mostly
    water, into a mulberry mass,
moulding calcium,

carbon, even gold, magnesium and such,
    into a chattering self tangled
in love and work,

scary dreams, capable of eyes that can see,
    only by moving constantly,
the constancy of things

like Stonehenge or cherry trees;

add uncle's eleven fingers
    making shadow-plays of rajas
and cats, hissing,

becoming fingers again, the look
    of panic on sister's face
an hour before

her wedding, a dated newspaper map
    of a place one has never seen, maybe
no longer there

after the riots, downtown Nairobi,
    that a friend carried in his passport
as others would

a woman's picture in their wallets;

add the lepers of Madurai,
    male, female, married,
with children,

lion faces, crabs for claws,
    clotted on their shadows
under the stone-eyed

goddesses of dance, mere pillars,
    moving as nothing on earth
can move—

I pass through them
    as they pass through me
taking and leaving

affections, seeds, skeletons,

millennia of fossil records
    of insects that do not last
a day,

body-prints of mayflies,
    a legend half-heard
in a train

of the half-man searching
    for an ever-fleeing
other half

through Muharram tigers,
    hyacinths in crocodile waters,
and the sweet

twisted lives of epileptic saints,

and even as I add,
    I lose, decompose
into my elements,

into other names and forms,
    past, and passing, tenses
without time,

caterpillar on a leaf, eating,
    being eaten.

Ecology

The day after the first rain,
for years, I would come home
in a rage,

for I could see from a mile away
our three Red Champak trees
had done it again,

had burst into flower and given Mother
her first blinding migraine
of the season

with their street-long heavy-hung
yellow pollen fog of a fragrance
no wind could sift,

no door could shut out from our black-
pillared house whose walls had ears
and eyes,

scales, smells, bone-creaks, nightly
visiting voices, and were porous
like us,

but Mother, flashing her temper
like her mother's twisted silver,
grandchildren's knickers

wet as the cold pack on her head,
would not let us cut down
a flowering tree

almost as old as her, seeded,
she said, by a passing bird's
providential droppings

to give her gods and her daughters
and daughters' daughters basketfuls
of annual flower

and for one line of cousins
a dower of migraines in season.

No Amnesiac King

One knows by now one is no amnesiac
king, whatever mother may say or child believe.

One cannot wait any more in the back
of one's mind for that conspiracy

of three fishermen and a palace cook
to bring, dressed in cardamom and clove,

the one well-timed memorable fish,
so one can cut straight with the royal knife

to the ring waiting in the belly,
and recover at one stroke all lost memory,

make up for the years drained in cocktail glasses
among dry women and pickled men, and give back

body to shadows, and undo the curse
that comes on the boat with love.

                         Or so it seems,

as I wait for my wife and watch the traffic
in seaside marketplaces and catch

my breath at the flat-metal beauty of whole pomfret,
round staring eyes and scales of silver

in the fisherman's pulsing basket,
and will not ask, for I know I cannot,

which, if any, in its deadwhite belly
has an uncooked signet ring and a forest

legend of wandering king and waiting
innocent, complete with fawn under tree

and inverse images in the water
of a stream that runs as if it doesn't.

In the Zoo

a tour with comments

And these
these are scavenger birds
                              fit emblems
for a city like Calcutta
or Madurai
crammed to the top of its gates

They are known generally
as adjutant storks
                          yes they have a long-legged dignity
that's slightly vulgar

Adjutant storks come in three shades
a faded black
                          like Madras lawyers   *a grey*
a dirty white
                          like grandmother's maggoty curds

They are rather noisy and heavy
in their take-off
and flap themselves into air
                              like father
into the rain, his baggy umbrellas with three ribs
broken by his sons in a fencing match and three
by last year's winds

But once air-borne
                          this furry spider-legged auntie
of a bird
            it circles
on motionless wings

        filling the sky's transparency
with slow sleepy perfect circles
like father's Magic Carpet story
that rowdy day when the rainstorm leaked
through the roof
and mother was ill
and he had to mop
the kitchen of our pattering feet

Questions

Two birds on the selfsame tree:
one of them eats the fruit of the tree,
the other watches without eating.
                        Mundaka 3.1.1

I

Eating, being eaten,
   parts of me watch, parts of me burn,
rarely a clear blue flame

without a sputtering of questions:
   why now, why here, why the Down's
syndrome

in the genes of happiness,
   the dead twin's cord of birth
noosed

around his brother's neck,
   a favourite dog eating puppies
in the garden,

why the fall into bliss on a cloudy afternoon?

Under the grey rains of June,
   in the black patience of stone elephants,
were the watchers there

with me, being born over and over, tearing
   each time through a waterbed paradise,
the original ocean

of milk, gills for lungs, the whole body
   a sucking at the nipple, a past perfect
of two in one,

my head's soft crown bathed in mother's blood,
   wearing tatters of attachments, bursting
into the cruelties

of earthly light, infected air?

Fear

For you, fear
is Terror,

wound museums
of Hiroshima,

the smell
of cooking

in Dacca sewers,
Madame Nhu's

Buddhist barbecues;
that well-known child

in napalm flames
with X-ray bones

running, running,
a stationary march

in the rods
and cones

of everyone's
Reuter eyes.

My fear,
small,

is a certain knock
on the backdoor

a minute
after midnight,

thirty years ago
or anytime now;

or a tiny
white lizard,

its stare, deadsnake
mouth,

and dinosaur
toes,

flattened to a fossil
in the crease

of my monkey cap
by my rolling,

sleeping, ignorant
skull.

Astronomer

Sky-man in a manhole
with astronomy for dream,
astrology for nightmare;

fat man full of proverbs,
the language of lean years,
living in square after

almanac square
prefiguring the day
of windfall and landslide

through a calculus
of good hours,
clutching at the tear

in his birthday shirt
as at a hole
in his mildewed horoscope,

squinting at the parallax
of black planets,
his Tiger, his Hare

moving in Sanskrit zodiacs,
forever troubled
by the fractions, the kidneys

in his Tamil flesh,
his body the Great Bear
dipping for the honey,

the woman-smell
in the small curly hair
down there.

Death and the Good Citizen

I know, you told me,
    your nightsoil and all
your city's, goes still
    warm every morning
in a government
    lorry, drippy (you said)
but punctual, by special
    arrangement to the municipal
gardens to make the grass
    grow tall for the cows
in the village, the rhino
    in the zoo: and the oranges
plump and glow, till
    they are a preternatural
orange.

Good animal yet perfect
    citizen, you, you are
biodegradable, you do
    return to nature: you will
your body to the nearest
    hospital, changing death into small
change and spare parts;
    dismantling, not de-
composing like the rest
    of us. Eyes in an eye bank
to blink some day for a stranger's
    brain, wait like mummy wheat
in the singular company
    of single eyes, pickled,
absolute.

Hearts,
      with your kind of temper,
   may even take, make connection
with alien veins, and continue
   your struggle to be naturalized:
beat, and learn to miss a beat
   in a foreign body.
            But
you know my tribe, incarnate
   unbelievers in bodies,
they'll speak proverbs, contest
   my will, against such degradation.
Hidebound, even worms cannot
   have me: they'll cremate
me in Sanskrit and sandalwood,
   have me sterilized
to a scatter of ash.

          Or abroad,
they'll lay me out in a funeral
   parlour, embalm me in pesticide,
bury me in a steel trap, lock
   me out of nature
till I'm oxidized by left-
   over air, withered by my own
vapours into grin and bone.
   My tissue will never graft,
will never know newsprint,
   never grow in a culture,
or be mould and compost
   for jasmine, eggplant
and the unearthly perfection
   of municipal oranges.

The Watchers

Lighter than light, blowing like air
   through keyholes, they watch without questions,
the watchers,

   they watch even the questions, as I live
over and over with cancelled stamps,
   in verandas,

Poonas, bus burnings, Chicagos
   near a backyard well of India
smells, basements,

   small back rooms, upstairs, downstairs,
once even under the stairs
   on election day,

with a dog who groaned human in his sleep
   and barked at spiders.

2

2

They impose nothing, take no positions.
    It's the mark of superior beings,
says the Book

    of Changes, they can watch a game of chess
silently. Or, for that matter,
    a Chinese wall

cemented with the bonemeal of friends
    and enemies. Unwitting witnesses,
impotence

    their supreme virtue, they move only
their eyes, and all things seem to find their form.
    Mere seers,

they make the scene.

Snakes and Ladders

Losing everytime I win, climbing
   ladders, falling to the bottom with snakes,
I make scenes:

in my anger, I smash all transparent
   things, crystal, glass panes, one-way mirrors,
and my glasses,

blinding myself, I hit my head on white
   walls, shut myself up in the bathroom,
toying with razors,

till I see blood on my thumb, when I
   black out, a child again in a glass booth
elevator, plummeting

to the earth five floors a second,
   taking my sky, turning cloud, and San Francisco
down to the ground,

where, sick to my stomach, I wake
   wide open, hugging the white toilet bowl,
my cool porcelain sister.

Pleasure

A naked Jaina monk
ravaged by spring
fever, the vigour

of long celibacy
lusting now as never before
for the reek and sight

of mango bud, now tight, now

loosening into petal,
stamen, and butterfly,
his several mouths

thirsting for breast,
buttock, smells of finger,
long hair, short hair,

the wet of places never dry,

skin roused even by
whips, self touching self,
all philosophy slimed

by its own saliva,
cool Ganges turning
sensual on him,

smeared his own private

untouchable Jaina
body with honey
thick and slow as pitch,

and stood continent
at last on an anthill
of red fire ants, crying

his old formulaic cry

at every twinge,
'Pleasure, Pleasure,
Great Pleasure!'—

no longer a formula
in the million mouths
of pleasure-in-pain

as the ants climb, tattooing

him, limb by limb,
and covet his body,
once naked, once even intangible.

A Poor Man's Riches 1

Winter is inventory time
  for toilet bowls in the hardware store;
in medical schools,

  for the hundred muscles you move
to stand perfectly still; in offices
  of immigration,

for coloured and discoloured aliens, brown
  eyes, father's name, five moles
classified

  in each oblong of visa and passport,
with only the pink, yellow, and green
  of a mango

from Acapulco to change the colours
  of poverty under the sweating
boiler pipes.

On the Death of a Poem

Images consult
one
another,

a conscience-
stricken
jury,

and come
slowly
to a sentence.

A Poor Man's Riches 2

Yet in April, between the lines
of classified ads, it's spring,
dogwood blows white

under a blight of elms, haiku
butterflies sleep in the ear
of a ruined Buddha,

and we steal kisses, committing grand
larceny under the boiler pipes
and I discover

at last how a woman is made
as she laughs and makes a man
of me,

teaches me combinations, how to pick
locks to raid her richest furs,
and loot the mint

of gold and silver even as they turn
into common money, leaving
mouth marks,

lowtide smells, and fingerprints
for all to see
in the secret accounts of joy.

A Minor Sacrifice

(remembering the dead in My Lai 4)

i

I'd just heard that day
of the mischievous king in the epic
who kills a snake in the forest
and thinks it would be such fun
to garland a sage's neck
with the cold dead thing,
and so he does,
and promptly earns a curse,
an early death by snakebite.

His son vows vengeance
and performs a sacrifice,
a magic rite
that draws every snake from everywhere,
till snakes of every stripe
begin to fall
through the blazing air
into his altar fires.

Then that day, Uncle, of all people,
a man who shudders at silk,
for he loves the worm,
who would never hurt a fly
but catch it most gently
to look at it eye to eye
and let it go,

suddenly strikes our first summer scorpion
on the wall next to Gopu's bed
with the ivory dragonhead

of his walking stick
and shows us the ripe
yellow poison-bead
behind the sting.

Grandmother then, tut-tutting
like a lizard,
tells us how a pregnant scorpion
will look for a warm secret place,
say, a little girl's underwear
or a little boy's jockstrap,
and then will burst her back
to let loose in her death
a host of baby scorpions.

'They're quite red at birth,
the little ones', Uncle says.
'They glow like hand-carved rubies
from Peking, redder than garnet,
especially when you hold them up
to the light.
And when they grow big,
they take on the colour of gray
China jade. Beautiful, beautiful',
he says, shaking his marmoset head.

ii

That afternoon, Shivanna asks me
under the sighing neem tree,
'Wouldn't you like to rid the world
of scorpions, if you could?'

'Yes, but how?'
                     'Witchcraft', says he,
shining darker than an ebony turtle.
'We can make them come at our bidding
when the sun is in Scorpio,
like guests to a wedding,
into the bole of this very tree.
And they will burn in a bonfire
you and I will light.'

                  'What, all of them?'
'Yes, and every kind. Black, red,
white, yellow, young, old,
the three-legged and the blind.'

'Can we do it now?'
                  'Not so fast, kiddo.
What can you get without a sacrifice?
First, we've to feed
the twelve-handed god of scorpions
something he loves as other gods
love goats and rice.
For that you need
one hundred live grasshoppers
caught on a newmoon Tuesday.
But remember: no wings on those things.
Catch them next Tuesday,
and I'll show you twigs on this tree
that will drip with scorpion legs.'

'Will you come with me?'
                                'No', he says.
'I'm busy. Take Gopu with you.
You'll need three jars.'

iii

So we steal three pickle jars at dawn
on that breezy newmoon Tuesday.
Leaping and hopping all over the lawn,

we become expert by noon
at the common art
of catching grasshoppers on the wing,

learning by the way
to tell apart
twigs and twiglike insects

that turn slowly round the twigs,
shamming dead
at the touch of a mere look,

as if it could burn.

We unlearn
what we couldn't have in years,
some small old fears

of other living things,
though we're still squeamish
when we pull off their wings

and shiver a bit
as we put away
those wriggles in our bottles.

And we learn,
as from no book,
the difficult art of counting

little writhing objects
through glass walls
with flaws and bubbles.

They had tiny compasses for thighs,
and moviestar goggles
for eyes.

iv

By evening we have ninety-nine.
The hardest is the last,
maybe because they too are learning.

But Gopu, who knows by heart the score
of every Test Match,
stalks and pounces in the half dark.

Breathless, he almost crushes his catch.
So we make our century,
sneak by the backdoor

to the bath house
to scrub and scour with coconut fibre
till the skins of our palms come off.

That night we don't eat or sleep too well.
We draw sticks and it falls to Gopu's lot
to keep the jars of grasshopper cripples safe

under his bed
and even that savage innocent
dreams all night

of every punishment
in the narrow woodcut columns
of the yellowing almanacs of Hindu hells.

v

When we go to see Shivanna
on Wednesday morning,
the jars behind our backs,
most of the grasshoppers
rather still or very slow,

Shivanna's mother tells us
he is in the hospital
taken sick with some strange
twitching disease.
We never see him alive again.

Uncle says, later,
    'Did you know, that Shivanna,
he clawed and kicked the air
all that day, that newmoon Tuesday,
like some bug
on its back?'

Alien

A foetus in an acrobat's womb,
   ignorant yet of barbed wire
and dotted lines,

hanger-on in terror of the fall
   while the mother-world turns somersaults,
whirling on the single bar,

as her body shapes under water
   a fish with gills into a baby
with a face

getting ready to make faces,
   and hands that will soon feel the powder touch
of monarch butterflies,

the tin and silver of nickel and dime,
   and learn right and left to staple, fold
and mutilate

a paper world in search of identity cards.

Saturdays

Enter a five-cornered room.
See yourself as another,
an older face in the sage
blue chair, the whole room
turning a page:
white words in black stone,
you know without knowing how
death will fog
a Saturday at three-fifteen
at home in a foreign place
where you jog,
as gold needles of rain
scatter the Art Fair in the park.

Not on Thursday, not in Paris
at nightfall,
not in a local train as you'd like
but on a day like this,
three weeks into a garbage strike,
a Dutch elm dying against a redbrick wall
that you'll remember but not know why
looking into a sawtooth
sky in a sequoia forest.
The two fingers you learned to pop
on your sixth birthday
crook and ache now,
like mother's on her sixtieth.
She died in the kidney wing, hallucinating.

A brother's briar pipe chatters
between his teeth,
as his heart comes to a stop,
accepting failure
that first Saturday in April,
mouth filled with bile
in a green-walled hotel room
within earshot of the Bombay sea
after a meeting under a slow ceiling
fan, red tea, letters
melting in alphabet soup
in the Reserve Bank,
his last thoughts like coils of brown rope
down his village well, sand, rope of sand.

The body we know is an almanac.
Saturdays ache
in shoulder bone and thigh bone,
dim is the Saturday gone
but iridescent
is the Saturday to come:
the window, two cherry trees,
Chicago's four November leaves,
the sulphuric sky now a salmon pink,
a wife's always clear face
now dark with unspent
panic, with no third eye, only a dent,
the mark marriage leaves on a small forehead
with ancestors in Syria, refugees

from Roman Saturdays.
The kettle's copper, mottled with water spots,
whistles in the kitchen. You
stir and leave the five-cornered room,
left foot wronged in a right-foot shoe,
imprisoned in reverse
in the looking-
glass image of a posthumous twin.

Turn around
and see the older man in the sage
blue chair turn around
to walk through the hole in the air,
his daily dying body
the one good omen
in a calendar of ominous Saturdays.

Zoo Gardens Revisited

Once flamingoes reminded me of long-legged aunts in whit
cottons, and black-faced monkeys of grave lowbrow uncles wit
movable scalps and wrinkled long black hands. Now animals remin
me only of animals,

orangutans of only orangutans, and of tuber
culosis in the Delhi Zoo. And the symmetric giraffe in Londo
that split in two trying to mount a coy female who gave him n
quarter.

Visitors no longer gape at ostriches, so they tell me, bu
shrewdly set their tail feathers on fire with lighter fluid an
cigarette lighters. So ostriches in zoos no longer hide the
heads in sand as they do in proverbs.

Some, they say, feed bananas to the dying race of ring
tailed monkeys, bananas with small exquisite needles in them. S
monkeys in zoos no longer eat bananas as they still do in templ
cities and Jungle Books.

Tigresses, I hear, go barren, or superintended by curiou
officials adulterate their line with half-hearted lions to bree
experimental ligers and tions as they breed pomatoes and totatoe
in botanical gardens.

Eight-foot tigers yawn away their potency. Till yesterday
they burned bright in the forests of the night. It was a way o
living. Now their eyes are embers in the ash. A slight movemer
of the eyelash flicks the ash.

The other day in Mysore a chimp named Subbu was paralysed ⸤ck down. He couldn't lift his chipped blue enamel mug to his ⸤ps and slurp his tea any more nor pout his lips to puff at his ⸤gar.

The Society of Animal Lovers babysat for Subbu in shifts ⸤ll in the small hours of the third morning he bit the sweetest ⸤dy of them all in a fury his protectors could not understand.

Lord of lion face, boar snout, and fish eyes, killer of ⸤ller cranes, shepherd of rampant elephants, devour my lambs, ⸤evour them whole, save them in the zoo garden ark of your belly.

Son to Father to Son

i

I am five,
I too dream of father,
   his beard a hanging hive,
turning slowly in his bed.
I scream at the hair
   on his hands
as they hold me close
to ask me why.

Sister swinging high
on the creaky swings,
   a window full of bees,
I could not tell him
his toes were talons,
   curving long
and slow
towards my sleep.

ii

It is no dream
to see a son skewered
   by a bamboo arrow
in a jungle trap;
or a daughter lowered
   like a match
into a sulphur mine
of hungry men.

I wake with a round
shadow for my head,
   the ceiling a falling
omen. A son's tall body
stands target at the door
   to ask me why
I keep so still and low.
How can I tell him

I see him shot,
washed, eyes shut,
   laid out,
I hear his cradle rock,
watch his ten little toes
   accuse my ceiling?

Drafts

A rough draft, getting rougher:
   a struggle in the crowd to see
the well-known

but half-seen Hyde Park rapist's face,
   half-seen perhaps only by another,
unseen

because seen too often; now towards,
   now away from what one thought
one always knew

without the help of policemen's
   drawings, a trayful of noses
and cruel lips.

2

Itself a copy of lost events,
   the original is nowhere, of which things,
even these hands,

seem but copies, garbled by a ciphered
   script, opaque as the Indus,
to be refigured

from broken seals, headless bodies,
   mere fingers, of merchants and dancers
in a charred city

with sewers, bath houses, a horned god
   of beasts among real homebodies,
family quarrels,

itches, clogs in the drain, the latter
   too ordinary to be figured
in the classic seals.

3

And we have originals, clay tigers
   that aboriginals drown after each small-
pox ritual,

or dinosaur smells, that leave no copies;
   and copies with displaced originals
like these words,

adopted daughters researching parents
   through maiden names in changing languages,
telephone books,

and familiar grins in railway stations.

4

The DNA leaves copies in me and mine
   of grandfather's violins, and programmes
of much older music;

the epilepsies go to an uncle
    to fill him with hymns and twitches,
bypassing me for now;

mother's migraines translate, I guess,
    into allergies, a fear of black cats,
and a daughter's passion

for bitter gourd and Dostoevsky;
    mother's almond eyes mix with my wife's
ancestral hazel

to give my son green flecks in a painter's eye,
    but the troubled look is all his own.

At Forty,

our Jatti, palace wrestler of Mysore,

teacher at the gym, has the grey
eyes of a cat, a yellow moustache,
and a whorl of tabby hair
on his chest.

No shirts under his military pea-coat
except on special days, when he wears
ribbons, medals and stripes—his father's
from World War One.

Someone in the palace is said to have said
one day, 'Jatti, the Wrestler, our teacher at the gym,
is now in top form, our state's very best',
and so they trim

his hair, give him all-body shaves to bring out
the fury of his yellow moustache.
Eggs and meat for breakfast, massages
of iguana fat,

till he glows in the dark, a lit medallion
figure. No sex, they whisper, for even
a look at your wife or that rumoured Muslim mistress
will drain

your power, loosen your grip. They weigh him,
measure his chest, his belly, his thigh,
and they pat his treasure. One April day,
they take him out

in a procession of purple turbans,
urchins, and burnished brass, the raucous
palace band on hire, from clocktower
to market square

to the white ropes of the red arena
in the Town Hall, where he is thrown
round after round, rolled over, jeered at
by rowdies

and sat upon by a nobody from nowhere,
a black hulk with a vulgar tiger's name
strutting in pink satin shorts. Jatti,
the Wrestler,

our teacher at the gym, walks away,
shaking off a swarm of eyes and hands, walks fast
and slow, in white trunks and bare feet,
through backstreet mats

of drying grain, straight to the gym,
to the red earth pit where he'd sparred
all year. Neck-deep he buries his body
in familiar ground,

only his bloodshot eyes moving in his head
and sometimes his short-haired scalp,
tabby-grey; his moustache unwaxed, turned down,
caked with mud.

Five disciples, we fumble and exercise
under a dusty bulb with dumb-bells
and parallel bars, over and over,
all eyes,

not knowing where to look
or when to leave, till he suddenly
shakes his body free, showers at full blast
under the corner tap,

and gently booms, 'I've to go home, boys',
like every day, and leaves, never
to come back, but to become
a sulphurous foreman

in a matchstick factory, well-known
for the fury of his yellow moustache,
once Jatti, wrestler, our teacher
at the gym.

He too Was a Light Sleeper once

He too was a light sleeper once.

A chuckle in the hall,
the pulse in the neck of a bird
that felt like his own,
a bloodred beak in a lime
tree, a nightmare prince,
anything at all
could wake him to coffee and a mountain-climb
of words on a page.

But now, after sudden jail
and long exile,
fruitbats in his family tree,
marriage of his heart's
little bird
to a clawing cat,
cigarette burns
on children's most private parts,
and the daily caw
at the window
of quarrelling carrion birds,

he just turns,
champs a curse in his jaw
as he gathers his heap
of limbs to climb again to other slopes of sleep,

the iron taste of print in his mouth.

Highway Stripper

Once as I was travelling
on a highway
to Mexico
behind a battered once-blue
Mustang
with a dusty rear window,
the wind really sang
for me

when suddenly
out of the side
of the speeding car
in front of me
a woman's hand
with a wrist-watch on it
threw away
a series of whirling objects
on to the hurtling road:

a straw
hat,
a white shoe fit
to be a fetish,
then another,
a heavy pleated skirt
and a fluttery
slip, faded pink,
frayed lace-edge
and all
(I even heard it swish),
a leg-of-mutton blouse
just as fluttery.

And as I stepped
on the gas
and my car lunged
into the fifty feet
between me
and them,
a rather ordinary,
used, and off-white bra
for smallish
breasts whirled off
the window
and struck
a farmer's barbed wire
with yellow-green wheat grass
beyond
and spread-eagled on it,
pinned
by the blowing wind.

Then before I knew,
bright red panties
laced with white
hit
my windshield
and I flinched,
I swerved,
but then
it was gone,
swept aside
before I straightened up—
fortunately, no one else
on the road:

excited, curious
to see the stripper
on the highway,
maybe with an urgent
lover's one free hand
(or were there more?)
on her breast
or thigh,
I stepped again
on the gas, frustrated by their
dusty rear window
at fifty feet,
I passed them
at seventy.

In that absolute
second,
that glimpse and after-
image in this hell
of voyeurs, I saw
only one at the wheel:
a man,
about forty,

a spectacled profile
looking only
at the road
beyond the nose
of his Mustang,
with a football
radio on.

4

Again and again
I looked
in my rearview
mirror
as I steadied my pace

against the circling trees,
but there was only
a man:

had he stripped
not only hat
and blouse, shoes
and panties
and bra,
had he shed maybe
even the woman
he was wearing,

or was it me
moulting, shedding
vestiges,
old investments,
rushing forever
towards a perfect
coupling
with naked nothing
in a world
without places?

Middle Age

Vietnam eyes my children in the sandbox
   as she splatters my neighbour's tall blond son,
while Biafra gives me

potbellied babies with copper-red
   hungry hair, pellagra scales,
and perpetual pink eyes.

I hold them close from famine to famine
   looking for mothers and penguin nuns,
fighting off

their little mouths from my dry
   fatherly nipples.

2

Half a heart working, the other half
   waiting for an attack from behind
the railing,

all my computers housed in one left lobe,
   the leftover right a temple flagstone
with the temple gone,

keeping safe a nest of purple
   immortal worms from the local
one-eyed raucous crows

and imported Mexican toucans.

3

Reason, locked out of the chicken coop,
   fearful of eagles it cannot see,
pecks at causes,

looks for reasons, grain among pebbles;
   even my belief in unbelief,
that henpecked coxcomb,

crows piteously aloud for a crumb of faith,
   and I look around to see nobody
is watching,

even I, wedded to doubt
   and only married to a woman,
yield, resist,

but inch towards the gypsy tents
   of witchcraft, casting horoscopes
at nightfall,

and manage to think the zodiac
   circulates my blood, that I'm Pisces,
fish out of water,

and my love a motherly Cancer.

Extended Family

Yet like grandfather
I bathe before the village crow

the dry chlorine water
my only Ganges

the naked Chicago bulb
a cousin of the Vedic sun

slap soap on my back
like father

and think
in proverbs

like me
I wipe myself dry

with an unwashed
Sears turkish towel

like mother
I hear faint morning song

(though here it sounds
Japanese)

and three clear strings
nextdoor

through kitchen
clatter

like my little daughter
I play shy

hand over crotch
my body not yet full

of thoughts novels
and children

I hold my peepee
like my little son

play garden hose
in and out
the bathtub

like my grandson
I look up

unborn
at myself

like my great
great-grandson

I am not yet
may never be

my future
dependent

on several
people

yet
to come

The Difference

The women mould a core of clay and straw,
wind around it
strings of beeswax on which the men

do the fine work of eyes and toenails,
picking
with hot needles the look in the eyes;

cover it with a second shell of clay
and pour eight
metals through a hole in the head,

the same escape hole, some would say,
that opens
for the Hindu soul at death.

When they bake the pot of the inchoate god
it makes faces,
exchanging metal for wax, an eye

for an eye, changing its state
as it cools,
when they take a knife to it and hack it

in two to discover the gleaming god.
They leave in
the core of clay for the heavier gods,

or else they'll fall on their faces.

It's with leftovers they make horses, toys;
life scenes of women
pounding rice with lifted pestles;

boys; or a drummer girl playing
with both hands
the two-headed drum for two dancers

with long brazen necks, long legs, long hands,
arrested in a whirl.

ii

But I, a community of one,
mould
myself both clay and metal,

body shape and lips; do my dancers first,
jet bombers
and tiny Taj Mahals for tourists

these days, then come through pestles,
women,
and horses to the gods who will bake

only if time permits, if there's metal left,
and desire,
or if my children's quarrels need new gods

for playthings. But today, out of the blue,
when Vishnu
came to mind, the Dark One you know

who began as a dwarf and rose in the world
to measure
heaven and earth with his paces,

I found I'd just enough left to fashion
his big toe,
and as I stare at this left toe and toenail

weighing on my hand, I can tell perhaps
the height
of this image as elephant trainers can

the height and gender of a runaway
elephant
by the size of his footprint in wet grass,

but I know I've no way at all of telling
the look,
if any, on his face, or of catching

the rumoured beat of his extraordinary heart.

Dancers in a Hospital

1

Spinoza grinding lenses brings me
    into focus, and I see my small brown
hand as a species

of eternity, when I go head first
    through a blueblack windshield in a red car,
fleeing news of riot

in the black white city, waking
    not quite awake, not quite dead, coming out
garbled, with a thick tongue,

rinsing out with chemicals
    a catarrh of consonants, the vowels
a whistle in the nose;

the head a gauze cocoon of bandages,
    a chrysalis among thorn trees and nurses,
I think of flight

while my leg, a separate mummy
    in a hospital stirrup, dreams as if
under pentothal

of Naga dancers.

2

Underground trains jogging through my sleep,
    my time's hurrying chariots, always
behind me in my walks

to the grocery in Bombay or Moscow,
    a rattle of shaking jowls, midnight heads
in crumpled hats, wet

newspapers with a seepage of backpage
    news in international latrines,
with Reagan or Mao

under our feet.

Moulting

Moulting has first to find a thorn at a suitable height to pin and fix the growing numbness in the tail. Then it can begin to slough and move out of that loose end, whole though flayed alive.

That's how you see now and then a dry skin or two hanging, and you may be sickened for a minute by a thin old snake vacillating and pale on a black thorn, working out a new body on a fence you just defiled.

Lord of snakes and eagles, and everything in between, cover my son with an hour's shade and be the thorn at a suitable height in his hour of change.

Some People

Others see a rush, a carnival, a million,
why does he see nothing, or worse, just one:

a singular body, a familiar head?
You'd worry too, wouldn't you, if,

in a whole milling conference
on Delhi milk and China soybean, in all

that human hair, national
smells and international fragrance,

you saw your wife from another life,
wed and left behind in childhood,

now six weeks dead, yet standing there
in raw-silk sari, in sandalwood footwear?

Connect!

Connect! Connect! cries my disconnecting
    madness, remembering phrases.
See the cycles,

father whispers in my ear, black holes
    and white noise, elections with four-year
shadows, red eclipses

and the statistics of rape. Connect,
    connect, beasts with monks, slave economies
and the golden bough.

But my watchers are silent as if
    they knew my truth is in fragments.
If they could, I guess

they would say, only the first thought
    is clear, the second is dim,
the third is ignorant

and it takes a lot of character
    not to call it mystery, to endure
the fog, and search

the mango grove unfolding leaf and twig
    for the zebra-striped caterpillar
in the middle of it,

waiting for a change of season.

Looking and Finding

Looking for a system, he finds a wife. Was it Vallejo who said, 'How anger breaks down a man into children!'?

Searching for mankind, he travels third class, a carrier for flu, bedbugs, eczema, and anarchist ideas: loses friends who fear all symptoms, any contact with any contact with possible syphilis.

Dreams are full of enemies, bruises; his wife scrubs his chest with rough compassion and lysol. That evening he beats up his three-year old son for laughing at him.

A stillness haunts his walking, there's a fury in his sitting quiet. He can neither sleep nor wake from the one-legged sleep on this Chicago lake of yachts in full sail, herons playing at sages.

Having no clear conscience, he looks for one in the morning news. Assam then, Punjab now, finds him guilty of an early breakfast of two whole poached eggs.

Attacked and defended by dying armies, the wounds find no blood on him, his bathroom cupboard is full of unused bandaids.

Thirsty, he finds the red of the wine slimy with the blood of bees, the wetness of water mossy with the fibre of the disinfected worm.

Calves' teeth in the foaming milk rattle in his mouth. The sugarcane worker's sickle wheels in the candy, cuts the palate, slits the tongue.

O alewives floating on my poison lake, he cries at 3 a.m., I wish I could feed myself to your fellow fish on my dinnerplate.

Love Poem for a Wife and Her Trees

Dear woman, you never let me forget
what I never quite remember:
you're not Mother,

certified dead but living on, close
to her children, tinkling in glass-
bead curtains,

peacock patterns shivering in three cities.
You remind me of the difference
especially

on panic's zenith, on the unattended
Ferris wheel rickety in the wind,
lest I collapse

into a son, destroy the intricate
diagrams of Dravidian kinship
where triangles

marry only circles descended
from other triangles and circles
in the notebooks

of anthropologists sitting
on family trees, those topsy-
turvy trees

with their roots in heaven
and branches in the earth.

Dear woman, you remind me again
in unlikely places like post offices
where I lick

your stamps, that I must remember
you're not my Daughter, unborn maybe
but always

present: lest I, like your nightmare
father-king, try to save you from the world,
that Grisly Beard,

that phantom son-in-law, save you even
from your own heart's madness, save you
from all things

messy and fertile, from all images
but mine; lock you deep in my male
and royal coffers,

impregnable wombs of metal, and throw away
the key in the alligator moat.
Out of touch,

deprived of traffic, now an ant-world
down below, seen from a fortieth floor,
nose pressed to window,

in the safe custody of an anti-
septic bubble, your spinal cord
will wither—

that stem of all senses, that second tree
with the root at the top, branches branching
in limb and lung,

down to toe, hangnail, and fingertip.

iii

I forget at night and remember at dawn
you're not me but Another, the faraway
stranger who's nearby,

like the Blue Mountain tree in the cuttings
of my garden graft, or its original,
sighted once

up close in my telescope, seasoned and alive
with leaf, bud, monkeys, birds, pendant
bats, parasites,

patch of blue scilla lilies in its shade;
exotic who inhabits my space
but migrates

to Panamas of another
childhood; one half of me, often
occupying all,

yet ever ready to call a taxi
and go away; foreign body
with a mind

that knows what I'll never know:
languages of the deep south, weathers,
underground faults

in my own continent, mushrooms
for love and hate, backrubs and sinister
witchery, how

to buy the perfect pomfret for dinner
in a world of stranded fish,
or pluck the one

red apple in the garden for dessert
from the one tree that's not upside down,
its mother root

unfolding in the earth a mirror image
of every branch and twig thrust deep
into the sky.

iv

Yet I know you'll play at Jewish mama,
sob-sister, daughter who needs help
with arithmetic,

even the sexpot nextdoor, topless
tree spirit on a temple frieze,
or plain Indian wife

at the village well, so I can play son,
father, brother, macho lover, gaping
tourist, and clumsy husband.

Looking for the Centre

Looking for the centre these days
   is like looking for the Center
for Missing Children

which used to be here, but now has moved
   downtown to a new building, southwest
of the Loop,

kitty corner from the Second Chicago
   Movers, last room to the left on the fifth
floor. Ask there

for the Center, anyone will tell you.

Looking for the centre is a job
   for eccentrics who can feel the thirteen
motions of the earth

when they stand still in the middle
   of the market: you too feel the galaxies
moving, as they talk

about pebbles. That evening you open
   an old anatomy textbook where
pictures in flesh tones

unfold a human body, layer
   under layer, skin, muscle, ganglia
of nerves, branching red

80

or blue veins, stomach, liver, pancreas
  and spleen, but then you open that last flap,
under the crimson

pair of kidneys, you plunge headlong—
  dandruff, doubts, and all—into a map
of the heavens.

3

Intoxicated by the body's toxins,
  liquors brewed in gland and gonad,
a zilla spider

on LSD, I spin enormous webs
  in a Tahiti forest of April twigs,
unaware

in my ecstasy I'm not at the centre,
  do not feel the tug of spidersilk,
for the web

has gaps any moth can fall through
  to safety, and live on to make more moths,
to make more holes

in royal brocades, my routine
  symmetries blown by the carelessness
of simple chemistry.

4

Suddenly, connections severed
    as in a lobotomy, unburdened
of history, I lose

my bearings, a circus zilla spun
    at the end of her rope, dizzy,
terrified,

and happy. And my watchers
    watch, cool as fires
in a mirror.

Chicago Zen

i

Now tidy your house,
dust especially your living room

and do not forget to name
all your children.

ii

Watch your step. Sight may strike you
blind in unexpected places.

The traffic light turns orange
on 57th and Dorchester, and you stumble,

you fall into a vision of forest fires,
enter a frothing Himalayan river,

rapid, silent.

On the 14th floor,
Lake Michigan crawls and crawls

in the window. Your thumbnail
cracks a lobster louse on the windowpane

from your daughter's hair
and you drown, eyes open,

towards the Indies, the antipodes.
And you, always so perfectly sane.

iii

Now you know what you always knew:
the country cannot be reached

by jet. Nor by boat on jungle river,
hashish behind the Monkey-temple,

nor moonshot to the cratered Sea
of Tranquillity, slim circus girls

on a tightrope between tree and tree
with white parasols, or the one

and only blue guitar.

      Nor by any
other means of transport,

migrating with a clean valid passport,
no, not even by transmigrating

without any passport at all,
but only by answering ordinary

black telephones, questions
walls and small children ask,

and answering all calls of nature.

iv

Watch your step, watch it, I say,
especially at the first high
threshold,

            and the sudden low
one near the end
of the flight
of stairs,

        and watch
for the last
step that's never there.

Waterfalls in a Bank

And then one sometimes sees waterfalls
   as the ancient Tamils saw them,
wavering snakeskins,

cascades of muslin. Sometimes
   in the spray, living and dying children
tumble towards old age,

lovesongs, and Biafra, orchestras in bombsites,
   hunger's saints in the glasshouse alley,
and more children,

with a bentover grandmother, black
   and wrinkled as a raisin, working
between mother's labouring

thighs, in a corner room with steaming
   gleaming brass vats, and four lemons
for good omens.

As I transact with the past as with another
   country with its own customs, currency,
stock exchange, always

at a loss when I count my change: water-
   falls of dying children, Assam
politics,

and downtown Nairobi fall through me
   in Hyde Park Bank, as I rise among them,
mud on my nose,

a rhododendron rising from a compost
    of rhododendrons, chicken bones,
silk of girlish hair,

and the nitrogen of earthworms.

As I hear the waters fall, the papers
    rustle, and it's evening: a paralytic sadhu,
tapdancer of the St Vitus's dance,

knocking his steps out on the pebbles
    with no reflexes left in either knee,
lifts with his one good finger

his loincloth, and pisses standing
    like a horse on my childhood's dark
sidestreet, aiming his stream

at two red flowers on the oleander bush,
    as a car turns the corner.
Headlights make his arc

a trajectory of yellow diamonds,
    scared instant rainbows, ejecting spurts
of crystal, shocked

by the commonplace cruelty of headlights.

January here: a seven-day snowfall
    covers Chicago, clogs the traffic,
grounds the planes;

muffles screams, garbage cans, pianos;
    topples a mayor and elects another
who promises clearance

of debts and snowfalls with their silent
    white effects, tickertape on astronauts,
white flower on black thorn.

And my watchers watch, from their nowhere perches.

Second Sight

In Pascal's endless queue,
people pray, whistle, or make

remarks. As we enter the dark,
someone says from behind,

'You are Hindoo, aren't you?
You must have second sight.'

I fumble in my nine
pockets like the night-blind

son-in-law groping
in every room for his wife,

and strike a light to regain
at once my first, and only,

sight.